Copyright © 2025 Jennifer Jones
All copyright laws and rights reserved.
Published in the U.S.A.
For more information, email info@ninjalifehacks.tv
Paperback ISBN: 978-1-63731-966-6
Hardcover ISBN: 978-1-63731-968-0
eBook ISBN: 978-1-63731-967-3

Find the Elves on Strike lesson plans at ninjalifehacks.tv

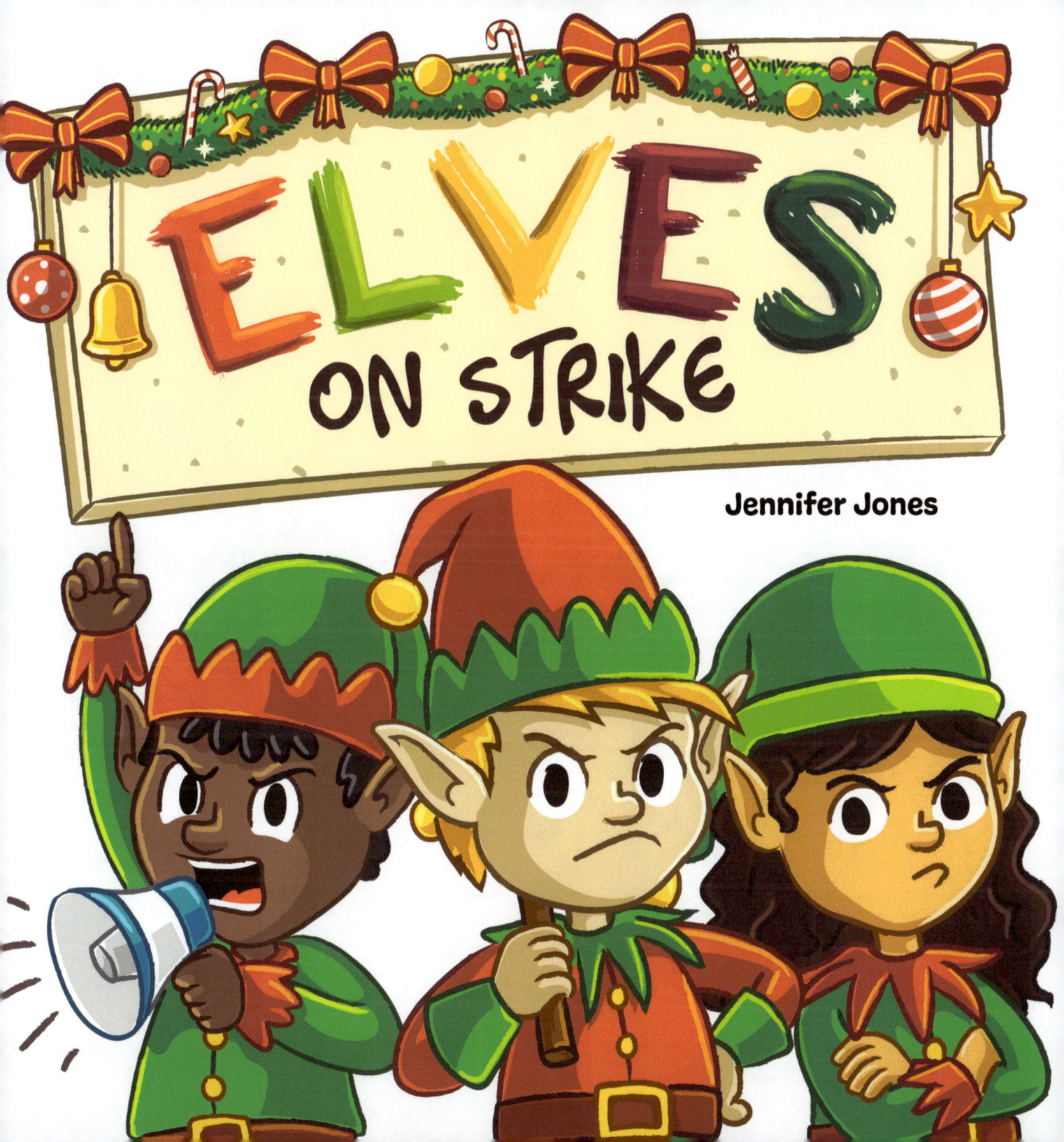

The snow was falling soft and sweet,
December had begun.
The elves were working night and day
with zero time for fun.

Then one cold morning at the Pole,
the workshop was a mess.
No elves, no bows, no jingle bells,
just piles of glitter stress!

Back at school, a letter came with sparkles down the side. It smelled like cocoa, looked hand-wrapped, and made Miss Holly wide-eyed.

We've worked so hard for years and years and barely get a break.
We just need rest and cookie naps for pepperminty sake!

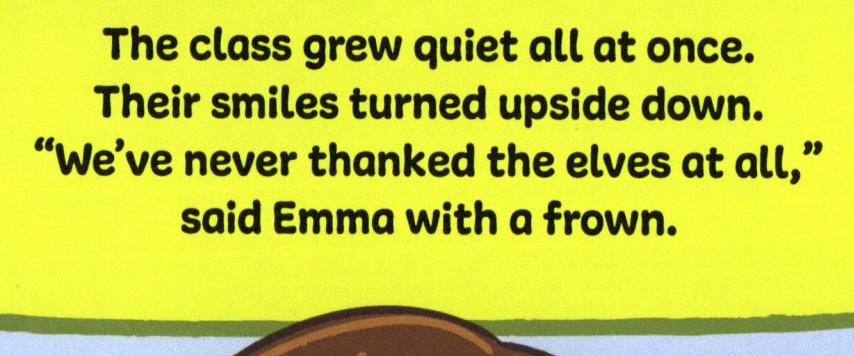

The class grew quiet all at once.
Their smiles turned upside down.
"We've never thanked the elves at all,"
said Emma with a frown.

I never even said thank you...

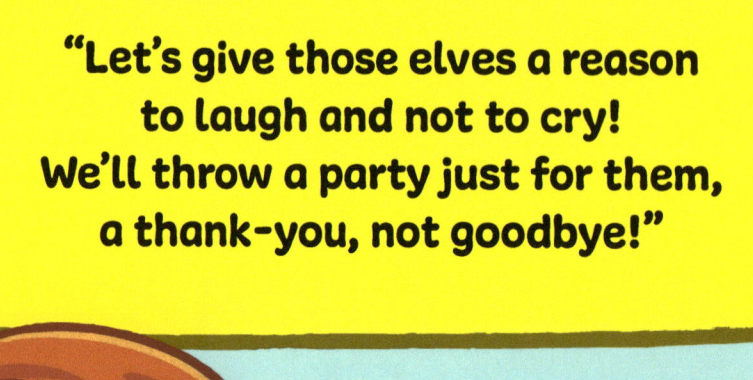

"Let's give those elves a reason to laugh and not to cry! We'll throw a party just for them, a thank-you, not goodbye!"

They baked the fluffiest sugar treats and hung up twinkle lights. They made elf beds with gumdrop foam for cozy winter nights.

Design Your Dream Elf Party!

What would you give the elves to say thank you?

Elf treat: _____
Fun activity: _____
_____
What I'd say to them: _____
_____

Draw your elf treat here!

www.ingramcontent.com/pod-product-compliance
Lightning Source LLC
Chambersburg PA
CBHW041712160426
43209CB00018B/1809